Title: List and Sell a Home in 7 Days Subtitle: Saves You Time. Sells More Homes. A Simple Proven System. Author: Landon Crigler

Introduction

Hello, I am Landon Crigler with Crigler Realty Group. **You do not know me**. That is exactly how I start every phone call to every listing prospect. (This will not apply to former customers-of course they know you and you can take a 1 year listing if you can) However even, then you should have a "seven day mind set." Why, Time is the stuff life is made of.

Please, let me tell you about my sales career. My first sales job was working for Sears in the tire department. They closed shortly after I left. I would like to think it was because I left. My humility, is only exceeded by my intelligence. This is a joke as you will find out. I had made up my mind to sell Real Estate. Surely if I could sell a set of 4 tires, selling 1 house would be a breeze. I interviewed the two largest firms (of course) in our small city. I went with the second company because I liked the Manager. David Clay. David was a kind principled man. He took care of his aged parents for most of his young life. After they died, he married a beautiful girl and has beautiful children. If anyone deserved happiness it was David.

Then the worst thing happened in my 40-year sales career. I **SOLD A HOUSE FOR CASH** my first week. "I knew it. This is easier than selling tires."

I said the worst thing because it fooled me. I did not sell a thing, nada, not one house in the next six months. My wife and 3 kids; especially my wife (kids will believe anything) wanted me to go back and beg Sears to take me back. I did consider it. However, something wonderful happened. The second thing happened to me. I found out that the Alabama State Docks in Mobile (pronounced Mo-Beel') was expanding and was go to take a whole neighborhood by **Eminent domain.** For those that haven't taken your real estate course; It is the government's legal authority to take **private property for public use**, provided that the property owner receives **just compensation.** That just compensation was in my opinion was 3 times the actual value of the home they were taking. This neighborhood had a high crime rate and was one of the lowest priced neighborhood in the city.

I decided to knock on every door in the neighborhood and ask had they heard they would have to move? Many were surprised others had heard about what was going to happen.

After asking and hearing their answer, I asked another question. Would you like to own a home that is worth at least twice what your current home is worth, in a neighborhood of your choosing, and have no monthly house payments ever again? What do you think most said; HE*L Yes! All you have to do is pick out the house you love and we will make a contract subject to you getting your money from the State Dock in 30 days. Most times the closing time on their home was less. Then we proceeded with their cash purchase of their new home. I sold 18 homes to people in that neighborhood, besides the other sales I made. I was rookie of the year. I went from the worst real estate salesman in the world to the best new realtor in our town! What was the second best thing I gained. **Where to look for business.**

What was the first best thing. Practice. Practice. Practice! It gave me 18 opportunities to gain experience. Ever since then I have never stopped learning. Here is a useful quote from Aristotle. "We **are what we repeatedly do. Excellence, therefore, is not an act but a habit.**"

Recently I have been **practicing** a **new way** of selling real estate; I call it **" List and Sell a Home in 7 Days." The word Sell does not mean close. But that accepted contract freezes the sale until closing.** I have sold over 1000 homes personally (very few of them in 7 days) Remember this is a new concept. But I have sold 3 my first month using this formula. I have never met these people before. I recorded a couple so you can see exactly how it worked. Here is a link..

I owned a mortgage company HHP Mortgage, I **franchised 4 other mortgage offices in 2 states**. They paid me exactly what I paid for a RE/MAX **franchise. $25000.00 each and 10% off gross income. We lost all of these during the crash of 2008; except one, Lan Mac Mortgage which was owned by one of the most knowledgeable, intelligent, and refined person you would ever meet; Barbara Lancaster of Lan Mac Mortgage. It is still operating today in Montgomery Alabama.**

I can confidently say there are very few people **in this world** that have been **involved in more real estate transactions (real estate sales and mortgage originations)** than I have on an individual basis. There was an old TV series "The Guns of Will Sonnet." They asked him (Will was Walter Brennan) if he was the fastest gun in the west. He answered "No, that would be my son John". So you are the second fastest gun in the West. He answered "No. That would be my second son Andrew." So You are the third fastest gun in the West. "I reckon so. **No brag just fact.**" This I believe is close to my situation. My 2 sons Walter and Mitchell are now better realtors and men than I ever was or hoped to be. I don't want to leave out my eldest son Cameron who is the manager of a large engineering firm in Mobile. Probably smarter in a way than any of us guys. Wy wife Debbie is the best of all of us in so many ways.

I'm not here to impress you. But, they tell me I must build credibility. This is the first book I have ever written. I don't know if it will sell or not. I want to show you what works "now" for me, and if you apply the things in this book **I firmly believe it will work for you.**

This book is based on another "7-day trial" that almost worked every time. The old pet store. You like has a certain dog in the store. The store owner says " Take him home for a week (7 Days) and if you don't like him bring him back," How many people brought that dog back. Almost none. You need to be that dog (excuse me ladies that beautiful French Poodle). How do you do that in real estate? You offer a "7 Day Listing" no strings attached. They will get attached to you if you **show them every step** you are taking in those seven days. Even if you don't sell the home in 7 days they may keep you. Doesn't that make sense. It is like the greatest college football coach Nick Saban said, "It's the process", that made his teams great. If you use **this process** outlined in this book the odds are you will become a great salesperson. You may be great right now. How about being great in less time. It is like in the movie The Count of Monte Cristo; Edmond Dantes assistant, Giovanni said "Let's kill them all and take the gold! What is wrong with this plan?" I am not advocating violence, but please "**Take the gold!**"

Caution! If you are not willing to call Expired Listings, Withdrawn Listings and "By Owners" save yourself some time and close this book. No one ever got a hit in baseball without stepping into the batter's box. If you can't handle rejection there are two things that you can do. 1. Quit! (most do) Or 2. Get better at handling them. I don't mean getting better at accepting rejection. Get better at getting to "yes." We will help you with that by you reading this book!

They tell me I should use the old school mantra.

- **Who**

- **What**

- **Where**

- **How***

- **Why**

- **When**

*Most of this book will concentrate on how? You may want to read the other sections first. Then read the "How" section. These are the details of this book. Your blueprint for success.

Section 1: Who" is this book for?

Experienced real estate agents. I have 47 years' experience in selling real estate and managing a real estate office. This is the **Most effective and Most time saving program** I have ever used. It is also the most recent I have used. It works now in today's real estate climate. I am not someone who tells you how to do something they have never done before. I am currently using the techniques in this book and succeeding. I use this 7 Day Mind Set for my existing past customers as well.

New agents. You can start this fast and even surpass experienced agents. Grandpa may have experience. What if 14-year-old Johnny and Grandpa saw Grandma having a stroke. Before Granda could find and open his flip phone, Johnny with the latest iPhone has located the number and called the local hospital. Finds directions on his phone and guides Grandpa as he drives Grandma to the emergency room where they are waiting for her. Knowledge of the newest tools wins out over experience many times. But if you have both; sorry Johnny Grandpa wins.

Those thinking about getting into real estate Please re-read the intro to this book especially the 6 month start of my career. This is typical. Over 90% of new agents fail in their first 2 years. You can hedge your bet by reading this book and you can hit the ground running if you apply what you learn.

Even FSBO's if you are selling your own home.

Section 2: "What" is the goal of this system?

Selling fast helps everyone. Sellers have less stress. You get faster closings. Buyers get the home they want quicker. It saves the stuff life is made of….. time. **I just did this experiment**. I Searched pending sales for 0 to 10 days on the market answer (drum roll) **150** that went into pending. I then searched pending sales 170 to 180 days on the market. Same number of days right? Answer**: 2.** That's right two. What? Yes . Which arena do you want to work in? **Which pond do you want to fish in? The one with 150 fish or 2 fish? Duh!**

In today's society everything is faster. Give the people what they want. You will be able to convince relatives, friends, or anyone else you contact to give you a chance. How? You have tools no one else has and you will give them a time frame no one else will give them. Wow what a Value Proposition. Here is an example of how many buyers **view the days** on the market of a property. Do you know why the bottom picture is better? "It has "a peal!" OK I am not a comedian, but I did sleep in a ditch last night. I mean at a Holiday Inn Express. View a listing as a banana.

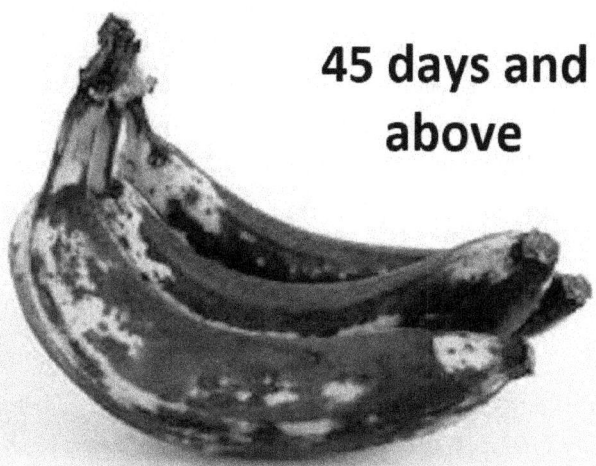

45 days and above

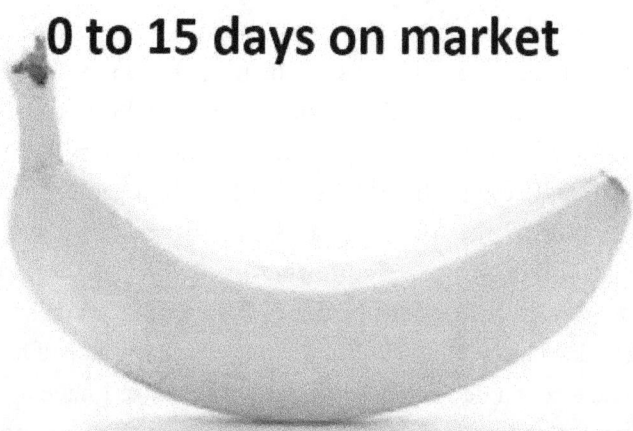

0 to 15 days on market

Section 3: 'Where" Do I get prospects?

!. Expired Listings MLS

I like to start with those that have expired 30 to 60 days. Why? First reason is that in the first week they possibly have been bombarded with other realtors telling them "I" can sell the home the other realtor couldn't. They still have a bad taste in their mouth. They are unlikely to jump back in with another realtor at this time. It allows them to possibly list on Zillow "By Owner" section (which by the way is hidden from the general public. They have to go through extra steps to get to the "For Sale By-Owner" section. They probably have views but no results.

This is where you step in. A 7-Day commitment will seem like a breath of fresh air, compared to the 90 to 180 day nightmare they had just 30 days ago. This is Landon Crigler with Crigler Realty Group, YOU DON'T KNOW ME. May, I ask you a couple of brief questions?" "Why do you think your home didn't sell?" "What do you think your agent could have done better to get your home sold? " Let them rant as long as they wish. "That sounded like an ordeal." "Are you still looking to sell your home?" They may say yes "Bur I am not ready to list with an agent." Translation "I am not ready to go back to Hell. You can say "After your experience I don't blame you one bit!" When you sell your home will you be moving to another city?" "Have you ever heard of a CRS Realtor? They are the PHD's of real estate. I can have one send you a list of homes that should meet your criteria. Would that be ok? May I get your email. that is how they send the **"new on the market home"** list." Another quick question. "Have you ever heard of a 7 Day Listing? Most people haven't, because realtors just don't do that. How long was your listing that expired ? "Do you know why I am willing to take a seven day listing?" No why? "Because I have **a system and tools that no one else has**. One tool allows me to text (5 times more effective than email) with **2 beautiful pictures** of your newly listed home, with an AI generated **killer description** of your home to (1000,2000,3000)or however many agents are in your MLS. I cannot list your home over the phone. May I send you a copy of an agreement so you can just look at it and see how it works in detail? May I have your email?" They normally reply "YES". Send through Dotloop (or whatever system you use). Have their signature already there. All they have to do is "click". Then you can send disclosures etc. Make it easy.

2.Withdrawn Listings MLS "I notice you withdrew your home from the market. May I ask a question? (Mother may I) Did you decide not to sell?" Wait. Wait. Wait. If they say yes; will you be selling in the future? If yes, make a note when they say and call a week before. If they no "we still want to sell." Then proceed with, "have you ever heard of a seven-day listing"? Then proceed with the above presentation.

3.For sale By Owner. Zillow The same presentation, except **I take the risk out** by taking an **exclusive agency listing**. "You can continue doing just what you are doing, and if you sell it within the next 7 days you owe me nothing." May I email you "a" copy of a listing to look at"? Notice the word "a listing" is not as threatening.

4.Relatives and Friends This should be easy. If a friend or relative will not give you 7 days, are they **really your friend or relative**? You do not have to answer that! Always remember, **a friend is one, who will stab you in the front!**

Do not make this your only source. Using the "You don't know me "phrase and closing the sale is a much more satisfying. If you do this, it is not your family circle that contains your market; it is another Circle. The Globe!

Section 4: "How" exactly do I do this? Here is the meat and potatoes!

How? Listing. The approach. Date do not Marry.

It starts with a mindset. Yours and your prospects. Let us start with your mindset. You may have been taught, that you should list a home for as long a period as possible. List it until the "sign rots." What does this do? It eases your mind. You do not want your mind eased. You want it to think at full throttle.

Have you ever heard about Parkinsons Law? It states, "Work expands to fill the time available for its completion." In simple realtor language.

- "If you give it 180 days, it will take 180 days. If you give it 7 days, it will get done in 7 days."

- "Work grows to fill the space you give it — so keep your space tight."

I recommend you postdate your listing for 2 days in the future. Why? One reason is it gives you time to get your ducks in a row. Photos, entering the listing into MLS, Disclosures, etc.

Now think about your prospect's mindset. They do not know you. They do not like salespeople. Especially the **expired listings and the withdrawn listings**; they have already heard the speeches about MLS, marketing, professionalism, and all of that meant "squat" to them because they were let down by their realtor's failure. You are not going to be that realtor.

That's why I start every call with "This is Landon Crigler with Crigler Realty Group you don't know me." Acknowledgement of the first fact eases their mind a little. Besides, they don't.

Another mindset is that of the seller whether they are a fsbo, expired, or withdrawn.

Let us start with the fsbo (For Sale by Owner). They have clearly shown they want to do this themselves. They want to remain single. So would you say I would like to marry you for six months! What are your odds of getting that listing on the first call? Nada, None, Zero.

You approach them after acknowledging they want to remain single. However, may I ask a couple of questions? Have you ever dated anyone? Sure. I don't want to ask you now, but may I just send you something about myself no obligation. In fact I will have **my driver take the Rolls Royce** and put it in your door. Would that be, ok? Please give me your address. (In your case the email). What are the odds that Person would say yes? Rather good.

What is your Rolls Royce? Here is my pitch to you. I provide A system (TextCatcher.com) that will deliver 2000 (or whatever the number of agents in your board) texts to the (device they check a minimum of 10 times a day) with 2 beautiful pictures of your home only. Texting is 5 times more efficient than emailing. 93% open rate. Most within 3 minutes. **No other realtor can do this for you**. They may start to believe, You are the Rolls Royce of realtors. They give you the go ahead on this "no risk" simple action. You can **use your old chevy** (your current email system Constant Contact, Mailchimp, or whatever system you choose to use to deliver the listing, There is a code you can use for your first texting session that will save you 50% off. We will walk you through it.

What is the package you deliver to them? A fully filled out sales agreement (except for no price) with the listing period being seven days. This gives you time to do a CMA (comparative market analysis). Does this make sense? You are on your way to the date. When you call after the email. I have done a little research on you. You are an extraordinary person. Again, we are talking about their home. Tell them all the good things you noticed. "I loved the way the office was set up. That was smart." May I ask How did you arrive at your price? This is critical. Diamond Jim Brady or Joe Girard (world's greatest car salesman) can't sell an overpriced listing, especially in 7 days. YOU MUST FIGHT FOR THE PRICE. Let me say this again. YOU MUST FIGHT FOR THE PRICE! Tell them "You don't get a second chance, to make a first impression." Don't give up too easily. If you must take the listing at a higher price and it hasn't sold after 3 days; approach them again for a reduction. Hopefully this will not be necessary if you took it at close to the CMA price.

What about expired listings and withdrawn listings? They have been married and divorced. It was messy. Call the same way. My name is_____ with _____ "You don't Know me." May I ask a couple of brief questions about your real estate? Are you still interest in selling?" Listen for response, if they say no move on, time is money. If they say yes, do not just jump in with your pitch. May I ask why do you think your home did not sell?" Let them talk about how the market was bad, the realtor did not communicate, etc." "How long was your home on the market?" You may know the answer but hear them out. Then they are primed for the pitch. "Have you ever heard of a 7-day listing. It is like a date instead of getting married. May I explain why I am willing to do what no other realtor will do." Then tell of the **immediate blast of texts** which is 5 times more effective than emails and tools that you have that other realtors don't. I cannot list your home over the phone. May I just send you a copy pf the listing agreement and you can look it over, May I get you email?" Wait for the response no matter how long it takes. If yes say In the meantime you can look at some videos of people that have used my service.

Call them back the next day. "Did you have a chance to look at the listing info I sent. If no, quickly say "I'll check with you in a few days." Then call the next day. If the answer is the same, ask "May I ask you how did you and the agent arrive at the price?" Whatever the answer ask, "May I send you an interesting chart on pricing?" Then send the pricing chart (download from me). Then send a copy of your CMA (Comparative Market Analysis). Then call back what did you think of the analysis? If he thinks it's too low ask, what price do you think it should be. If it is within 5% of your CMA say that sounds reasonable. Will you give me seven days to sell your home?…….. Wait, Wait, Wait. If yes just tell him to click the signature link you have sent through Dotloop or whatever other system you use. If he says " I need to think about it". Politely ask "What have you got to lose, 7 days." I really think I can do this. Can we go ahead? " You have earned the right by this time to have the listing. Keep politely going. "Can we work together OK?"

Here is a common objection. "I have a friend in the business." **Response** "They can still sell it if they are members of the MLS." Wait for a response; if they say I told him I would list with him. "Will their company even allow him(her) to take a 7-day listing? Most will not." So, they will not be able to do what I can do." What do you say, let me have just 7 days. Next offer Why don't you **just try me for just seven days** and if we don't get a contract, call him. If the home is higher in price , **offer a 25% referral** (last resort only), it is like a gift to them they won't spend any time, will get paid keep your friendship intact. If you list with him and he (She) doesn't sell it there may be hard feelings on both sides." It happens a lot. "May we go ahead today?"

The Price. Do a Killer CMA (Comparative Market Analysis) Fight for the Price

Every home is unique. That is what makes pricing a home so difficult. A car on the other hand always has 4 tires, 2 or 4 doors and it has an engine. Color does not make too much difference. Mileage can be adjusted. But every single home is unique. It is much harder to produce an expected selling price. That is why appraisal is an **opinion of value**. There are however some principals that you can use in making the best CMA (Comparative Market Analysis) you can. Here are a few guidelines that can help you.

!. If all other components are somewhat equal, you can subtract 1% home value per year of age difference. (**Less lot costs**. Land normally does not have wear and tear. It has existed for millions of years. That is a good warranty) Example $300,000 Total cost of new home and lot comparable. The lot cost $50,000, Your listing is 5 yrs old. Compared to a new home you would Take the Total $300,000 home price and deduct land value which would give you $250,000 less 5% (1% per year) = $12,500 . That would be a $300,000 less $12,500 = $287,500 Compared to a similar new home. Use this same formula for **any age difference** in your comparable Sales.

2. One Story against Two Story. Let's take the same example The 5-year-old home is a two-story 2000 sq ft total. 1000 sq ft on the first story and 1000 sq ft on the second story. 2 Of the most expensive components of a home are the roof, and the foundation. The first story does not have a roof. The second story does not have a foundation. Take 5% from the portion that is 2 story 1000 sq ft. 287500 x .5% = $143,750 times 5% = $7,188 So the price for the two story should be $287,500 less $7,188 or $280,312. I would suggest $279,900 as the list price. Also, the population is getting older. A high percentage of them will not buy a 2 story regardless of price. So even a lower price may be in order. Remember FIGHT FOR THE PRICE.

I am not an appraiser. However, giving an accurate CMA is a keystone in helping you sell a home in 7 days.

Here are a list of other considerations when doing a CMA

- Use Sold, Not Just Listed, Comparables – **Focus** on **recently sold properties** (ideally within the past 3–6 months). It is better to use what is happening now. The newer the comps the better.
- Stay Within a 1-Mile Radius (Urban) – Expand only in rural/suburban areas with similar market conditions.
- Match Style and Type – Compare like-for-like (ranch to ranch, condo to condo, etc.).
- Similar Square Footage – Use properties within ±15–20% of the subject's living area (GLA). The home has to be comparable size to be a comparable.
- Match Bedroom and Bathroom Count – Value can shift significantly with changes in bedroom/bathroom count. Not so much on bedrooms. Baths definitely.
- Time Adjust for Market Trends – Adjust older comps for appreciation or depreciation.
- Match Age of Improvements – Try to compare homes built within 10–15 years of each other. Guide 1% per year building only
- Include a Garage or Carport Comparison – Note garage type and number of bays. Double Garage can add $25,000 or more
- Adjust for Lot Size – Larger lots typically add value, but per-foot value declines. (don't just add value per foot) Not much of a factor in a subdivision)
- Consider Location Features – E.g., corner lots, cul-de-sacs, lake views, etc. (Corner lots not so much.)
- Note Renovations or Condition Differences – Remodels can greatly influence value.
- Use at Least 3 Good Comparable sales – 3 minimum for credibility; up to 5–7 helps refine accuracy.
- Avoid Outliers – Ignore extreme values unless clearly justified.

- Calculate Price Per Square Foot Carefully – Use only heated/cooled living area.
- Stay in the Same School District – School zones often have strong influence on pricing. Not a hard and fast rule.
- Consider Zoning and Usage – Compare only to similar zoning classifications.
- Note Construction Type – Brick vs. siding, slab vs. basement can affect value.
- Nail the price. $275,900 Some present a Value Range, Not a Single Price – If you choose to do this Provide a reasonable (very small) range based on market data. **"VRM"** my **most hated acronym** in real estate. Variable Range Marketing (Started I believe by Prudential). They and the MLS's that allowed it in my opinion should have been sued for billions of dollars. And that still wouldn't make up for all the **time lost by all the other agents** in showing overpriced homes or explaining to buyers what it meant. Example Sales Price $275375* * {The owner will consider offers from 275,000 to 375,000}. **Ridiculous!** Sorry Prudential agents, you may have gotten listings with this, but you and the rest of us have wasted a lot of time. Remember "Time is the stuff life is made of." **Maybe they should have had their agents read this book**.
- Start with good comparable homes. Preferably in the same neighborhood. If this is not possible look for a similar neighborhood with similar homes, Caution: **check lot value in the public records**. If the comparable properties have different Lot values you must adjust up or down for the difference.

Bonus tip. They say, "we can always come down on our price." No you can't. Show them the chart. If you price it too high you will **never see "Your Buyer"** he lives in the lower group. Then say **we can always go up!** What? Yes, if I have made the price too low there is a **good chance** we will get **multiple offers**. That's what we call a **bidding war**. Guess who wins this war? **YOU**. Yes you can go up." **Fight for the Price** !

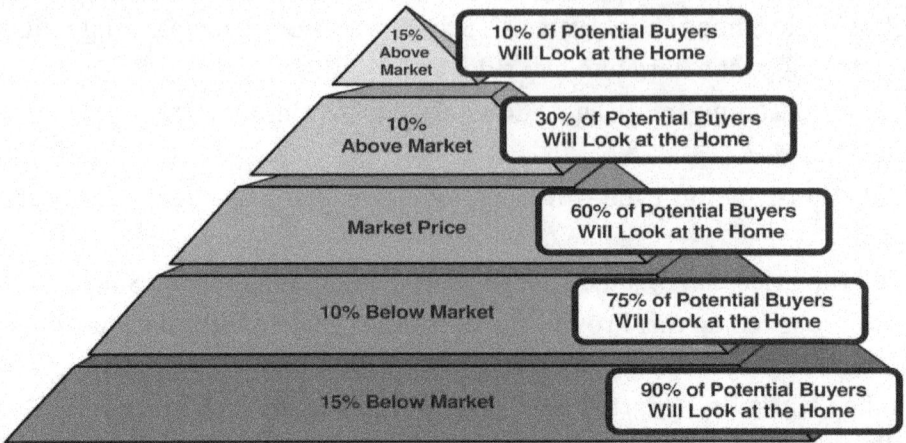

THE PRICING PYRAMID

- 15% Above Market — 10% of Potential Buyers Will Look at the Home
- 10% Above Market — 30% of Potential Buyers Will Look at the Home
- Market Price — 60% of Potential Buyers Will Look at the Home
- 10% Below Market — 75% of Potential Buyers Will Look at the Home
- 15% Below Market — 90% of Potential Buyers Will Look at the Home

ROYAL SHELL.

Inspections. The purchase agreement may be just the beginning.

I am mainly a listing agent; It seems as though the inspector's job is to **kill the sale**. You as a listing agent must deal with this adroitly. That is a big word for a ninth-grade graduate. Just kidding, I was a valedictorian of my preschool.

Anyway, enough about me. This could be a sticky situation. The seller loves this house; his daughter walked down those stairs to the prom. She was born there. Every great memory was made in this home. The inspector invariably says This home is "**CRAP**." The sellers are mad. The buyers did not realize this home was "**CRAP**." Both the **buyer's agent and the selling agent must prepare their clients**. Advise them both. They are **paid** to **make this home look like CRAP**.

Please don't take this personally. Most of them worked previously for **Roto-Rooter** where they dealt with real **CRAP** all day. So sometimes they cannot tell the difference. I don't think inspectors read this book, but if you do, you need to put some plus's along with all of the minuses. Please, Please, advise each party this is a real possibility. If it comes back **CRAP,** what can you do? 1.Fix the **CRAP.** 2. Agree to fix part of the **CRAP** or 3. Use the mustard on the prom dress approach. What is that? I am so glad you asked.

Pro Tip. What if the inspection comes in and the buyer wants everything fixed or a lower sales price. Some things may be in your contract that are agreed to up front. Components like heating and air shall be in working order at time of conveyance. How to you handle this? If they have countered their offer with all kinds of repairs like replace this replace that. What can you do? I have a story I tell.

It is called "Mustard spot on the Prom Dress. Sally is a hugely popular girl in Ridgemont High. Mike knows this and as soon as the date for the prom is announced he rushes to contact Sally and asks her to go. She is modest and thinks no one else will ask her. She timidly accepts. On the night of the prom Mike comes to pick up Sally. She spent days picking out the perfect dress. It is magnificent. She has been eating a delicious Oscar Meyer hot dog. She spills a little mustard on her prom Dress. She comes to the door and Mike (the neat freak) is horrified. Unaware she had the spot Sally says, "I will clean it up and I will be right back." Mike insists she put on a new dress, she can't possibly wear that one. Mike is unaware Harry Styles. Tom Selleck (my wife says he looks like he is in his 20's-I hate him), and Timothée "Tim-O-Tay"(sounds like the old Buckwheat skit on SNL) Chalamet; had all inquired about taking her to the prom. She told Mike to "wait in the car and give me a few minutes". The first call she made was to Harry Styles. Harry said "I would love to take you to the prom." She opens the door with a clean beautiful original dress and Mike said "That looks OK lets go." She said Harry Styles didn't ask me about my dress. He is picking me up in 10 minutes. Thanks but no thanks. If you had several people inquire about your listing follow up before to respond to the inspection contingency. To be fair tell the other agent what you are doing. You may be surprised at how much **the home improved** when they realize Sally(your beautiful home) is **back on the market** once that repair addendum was presented. This could be a lesson for you when you are representing the buyer.

Here is one for your buyer. There were two dogs, and they were best friends. Rough and Ready. Ready saw Rough and he looked terrible in fact he looked rough. What is the matter Ready? Rough said I have not eaten in days; I am starving, I just need a bone. Can you help me? Ready said, I am always ready to help a great friend like you. Ready looks all over searching near and far, east and west, and low and behold what does he see the thicket. A large, delicious bone. He was so excited. He grabbed the bone in his huge jaws and immediately raced to his friend Rough. Rough was so thankful that he cried. You are the best Ready, thank you so much. Rough put the bone in his mouth feeling his mouth start to water. I am going home, and this bone is going to save me. On the way home he has to cross a stream. As he was crossing, he looked down and what did he see. A haggard dog with a huge bone; it seemed much bigger than his. He decides he will swap bones with the other dog. He opens his mouth; his bone falls into the river and low and behold the other dawg (for Georgia fans) disappeared. Rough died on the way home. When you have an offer in hand that is good; don't go looking for something better and lose the prospect you have. **It may turn out rough for you.**

Selling. The Prequalification. Don't show until you know!

Start with this question. Have you been preapproved for a loan? Yes. May I ask your lender to send it to me? This will help if you decide to make an offer. Many companies require that before they present anything to their sellers.. If they answer no you may say normally my company requires a pre-approval letter; However since you are here, may I ask you a few questions that will help us both know that you can buy the home you choose. Would that be ok? You are so nice. Here are some of the most pertinent questions.

Before you start asking you should be aware of the 3 basic principles of lending. They are called the 3 C's.

Credit, Capacity, Collateral.

Credit What is your score? Why?

Let us start with a chart **you can use for the rest of your career**. Which score
would you loan money to? With a score below 600 there is a 1 in 8 chance
of foreclosure. Above 800 a 1 in 1292 chance of foreclosure.

• Credit Score	• Risk of Default	•
• Above 800	• 1292	• to 1
• 769-799	• 597	• to 1
• 720-759	• 323	• to 1
• 700-719	• 123	• to 1
• 680-699	• 55	• to 1
• 660-679	• 38	• to 1
• 620-659	• 26	• to 1
• Below 600	• 8	• to 1

So you ask for their credit score (if they are not paying cash) will determine right
away what you should do. If they say they are paying cash, get out the car
keys. If they can verify where it is coming
from.
Caution: If they have already been approved **don't do anything**. And tell them
don't apply for
any more credit or purchase any large item by credit.
There are a few ways you can counsel them if they do not qualify at this time. You
can put **them on lay-away**. If they have an installment (car note, Boat Note
etc. accounts that are not too high say $500.00 per

month or less, they can pay them down to 20% of the original loan and it won't
count against their score and will raise the score the next cycle. Or they can
pay a small fee to rescore sooner. If there are errors on their credit report
they can have
them removed with proof and get a rescore. Even if they qualify for a loan. A
higher score means a lower rate. You can be the hero, no, even a super-hero.
Caution: If they have already been approved, do not do anything. And tell
them do not apply for any more credit or purchase any large item by credit.

Capacity. Simply Can he afford this house?

Technically it is the ability of the buyer (borrower) to pay his mortgage payment
plus all his other obligations. In addition, he should have the capacity to
make the down payment (if required) and
closing Costs (if required). The factors that would come into play in making a
decision as far as the capacity is concerned are:

   a. Total Income
   b. Total Debt
   c. Total liquid assets for the down payment and closing costs.
These relationships are expressed as the "Housing Ration" and the total monthly
"Debt Ratio."

The "Housing Ratio" is expressed as follows:

Total housing payment(principal, interest, taxes, insurance, mortgage insurance(if
any) other (condo fees etc.) divided by the Gross Monthly Income.
         Here is an example $900.00 (total housing payment) divided by $4000
(Gross monthly income) = .23 or 23% This is good. There is no rule especially
with automated underwriting but if this is below 30% it is normally satisfactory.

The Total Monthly Debt Ratio is expressed as follows:
Total debt (Housing Payment plus certain other monthly debts. Example car
payments etc.) divided by Gross Monthly Income.

Example: $900.00 (Total Monthly Housing Payment) + Other monthly debts $500.00 divided by GRM $4000 = .35 or 35% The old guideline was 36% so we are close but should be all right if the credit and collateral are good.

Pro Tip. What income can you count? Use the Cha Cha method. One, two (step Back 2 years) Cha, Cha, Cha, (3 Years forward forward)
Generally, the person must have been at their job for 2 years. (Back) If they are a laborer, it can be for 2 or more employers. It must be continuous. A professional, such as an engineer, or a teacher, who graduated from college. They can go to work right away and qualify for most mortgage programs as long as it is in the field of their major. 2 years back for employment. College may count.
3 Years forward. Say a person is receiving child support. It must extend 3 years into the future. The same for a mortgage that they hold, and they have a history of receiving payments. They must extend 3 years into the future, just remember the Cha Cha. 2 steps back on employment 3 years forward on payments they receive must extend 3 years into the future before it can be counted as income on their mortgage application.

Collateral. What is it?
Let us talk about collateral: This would be the **subject property**. Is the value of the subject property enough to justify the loan that the buyer is applying for. What is the formula?

The loan amount divided by appraised value or sales price (whichever is lower) = Loan to Value or LTV

Example $150,000 Loan amount divided by $200,000 (Appraised value or sales price whichever is lower) = .75 or 75% LTV.
 In loans such as VA which can have a 0 Zero down payment the appraisal at least matching the sales price is critical. Many times the borrower is going VA because they have limited cash. It could blow the deal if the seller isn't willing to come down to the appraised value. That is where you as the sales person will earn your money. FHÀ is 3.5% down which could cause trouble as well if the appraisal comes in low. If you represent the seller make sure the home is in the best

condition so you can get the appraisal price the same or more than the sales price. Makes sense huh?

Pro Tip: What if the appraisal comes up short. Game over right! Wrong. There are a few things that you might do to save the sale. The easiest way of course is to lower the price. However, the seller may not want to do this especially if he has agreed to pay say $4000.00 in sellers costs. What else can be done. Another way that may be possible is to ask the buyer to raise the rate on their loan. What? Say the loan is $200,000. The rate is 6.25 %. The origination fee is 1% or $2000.00. If the appraisal came in $2000.00 short. The rate could be raised to 6.5% or 6.625% and the origination fee could be eliminated with the higher rate. The price could be reduced by $2000.00 and without the $2000.00 origination fee the closing costs would be reduced by $2000.00. Therefore the sellers contribution would drop to $2000.00 and the net return to the seller would be the same. Everyone's' happy right? Maybe not the buyer who has a higher rate. There is a phrase "Date the Rate Marry the home. You start out with a lower price on the home. In a year or two the rates may drop significantly and the buyer could refinance and actually lower the monthly payment. Also historically home values have increased. This is how you separate yourself from almost every other agent in town. This could also be used in reverse. If the home appraised for 2000 more you could raise the price and the seller could contribute more if the buyer was short on funds and could afford a higher payment. In either case you are the hero and you have a commission check in your pocket. If this **happened once** it would **pay for this book hundreds of times**. It certainly would be **worth a 5 star review**, don't you think. I would really appreciate it.

The Showing. How to show homes and save time (the stuff life is made of).

This 4-property rule applies to most showings. There is an exception. If the client is coming from out of town and they must make a decision within a couple of days. You show until death. Either yours or theirs. Don't let them leave town without an accepted contract. Even then I would start with this tried an proven method.

Let's understand the new law before showing a prospect a home. Here is a condensed version.

As of August 17, 2024, REALTORS® must have a signed written agreement with a buyer before showing any property, including virtual tours. This agreement outlines the services provided and specifies the agent's compensation, which must be clearly stated and not open-ended. This change, resulting from a legal settlement, aims to enhance transparency and ensure that buyers understand their agent's role and fees upfront .

With that out of the way. Let's learn a proven method

The showing order. Start with 4 houses you think they might buy. Be thorough. Ask a lot of questions before you show them. What price range? You may have to adjust this after a few questions. Ask! Ask! Ask! As many questions about their wants and needs in a home. You want as good a picture as possible to help them find the home they want to buy.

Here is a great example of showing order. After you have gotten the information from the buyer; choose the top 4 homes you think as a professional that fits their needs.

1. **The second to worst of the 4.** Why? You want to lower their expectations to start. Do not make it too bad.
2. **The second best of the 4.** Ah things are getting better. I like this one.
3. **The absolute best of the 4.** This is the home you feel they should buy. " This is it they may say." But they may say "each home is getting better, let's keep looking." At this point you may think "this will go on forever." Remember time is the stuff life is made of. We will stop the **hope train** with the next showing.
4. **The worst of the 4.** This will do 2 things; stop the showing train and heighten their love for number 3. Let us hurry before someone else snaps up your

perfect home. Yes! You have done it in record time. No need to repeat myself. Time is....you know what it is.

Doesn't this make sense? In a perfect world yes. However, we live in an imperfect world. Sometimes we must adjust our sails.

You may have read them wrong. After listening to them you may have to change course quickly. Immediately pull up new properties with the added information you have gained. Use the same order for the same reason as before.

Section 5: Why" Should I do this?

Benjamin Franklin said time is the "stuff" life is made of. Save part of your life and choose what you do with that part.

Would you rather work longer and make less or

Work shorter and make more. Duh! This system allows you to choose.

Once you master the 7 Day Listing, **you will never go back to 3 month or 6 month listings. Watch these videos of live calls. https://vimeo.com/1075301453**

Section 6: "When" Should I do this?

What keeps you talking yourself out of calling? Be honest. It is **fear of rejection**.

I remember knocking on a "For Sale by Owner" door. A beautiful little girl opened the door (she shouldn't have) I said my name is Landon Crigler with Crigler Realty Group, may I speak to mommy or daddy?" "She replied No .... **but I can reject you for them!**" Not a true story but you get the point. **Embrace rejection.**

Why? You can become immune, and it does not continue to control your actions. Here are a couple of quotes that may help you.

Walt Disney said, "The way to get started is to stop thinking and start doing" Call

Moses Maimonides said, "The risk of a wrong decision is preferable to the terror of indecision,"

Sophia Amoruso said, "Half of getting there is having the confidence to show up." Show up and start calling.

Pat Summit said, "Confidence is what happens when you have done the hard work that entitles you to Succeed."

Landon Crigler said, "A watched clock, never boils." Just checking, to see if you are still paying attention.

Fabricated excuses. "I need to wait on my perfect pictures." Ok, make a couple perfect ChatGPT modified pictures from Zillow or drive by photos on your cell phone. Then send texts now and add the rest after you've done your best.

I want to polish up my presentation. The best way to do that is to give them and examine what you can do better. Rinse and repeat. What could I have done better? Babe Ruth said, "Every strike out brings me one step closer to the next home run." Recreate every call in your mind. Copy Success. Ask yourself why, if you fail. Examine every step. Remember the Babe, every failure corrected brings you closer to Perfection.

Will you get discouraged in this business? Sometimes yes. But keep calling. Zig Ziglar said "Don't get discouraged; it is often the last key in the bunch that opens the lock," The key according to Esther Dyson is "Always make new mistakes."

One more for the road. The road to success, Robert Stauss said "Success is a little like wrestling a gorilla. You don't quit when you are tired – you quit when the gorilla is tired."

This is not a good time to call the prospect. Is **that your fabricated thinking** or the prospect's reality? They will let you know if that is true. **Call, Call, Call.**

Charles Dickens said," I never could have done what I have done without the habit of punctuality, order, and diligence."

There is a scripture in the Bible that I used to think of when I wanted to lie in bed and do nothing, "Yet a little sleep, a little folding of the hands to sleep: So shall thy poverty come as one that travelleth, and thy want as an armed man," Another version says "Your poverty will come like a bandit' and your want like an armed man."

A good simple slogan to get things done, "Do it Now,"

The biggest road block to success is PROCRASTINATION! The most important rule is to ask about how to handle any item you see. 4 Choices

1. Do it now-respond
2. Delegate- Hand it off to someone (or something auto responder)
3. Designate it -Take time to put it on a to do list or calendar
4. Discard it.- Trash it.

What are the things directly related to Listing and Selling real estate. Do those things first. Even if they are the hardest.

Sources

Most of the quotes cited are from a book called "Fired UP! Selling" by Ray Bard

Additional closes.

"Just one more thing before we hang up" Colombo Close. How about we try this for seven days and you can interview other agents or talk to your friend during that period. But imagine if I get a contract during those seven days, you'll be on your way to _____ without any more hassle. Can we go ahead? It's just 7 days.

I want to think it over. "Just out of curiosity what is it that holding you back?"

"Just out of curiosity what needs to happen for you to make a decision about this?"

Most people I talk to go ahead with me after we have talked this far. Can we go ahead.

Don't worry

"If you give me a try" I promise you want be disappointed.

Thank you so much for purchasing this book and taking the time to read it. As we said many times in this book Benjamin Franklin said "Time is the stuff life is made of." You have given me a part of your life (and a little money). It is my sincere hope that you have gained something from this book. I hope that what you have learned will repay you 1000-fold. Thanks, and happy selling. Landon